Other books by the Cheezburger Network:

I Can Has Cheezburger? A LOLcat Colleckshun

How to Take Over Teh Wurld: A LOLcat Guide 2 Winning

Teh Itteh Bitteh Book of Kittehs: A LOLcat Guide 2 Kittens

I Has a Hotdog: What Your Dog Is Really Thinking

Graph Out Loud: Music. Movies. Graphs. Awesome.

Fail Nation: A Visual Romp Through the World of Epic Fails

There, I Fixed It: (No, You Didn't)

FAIL HARDER

RIDICULOUS ILLUSTRATIONS OF EPIC FAILS

failblog.org community

Andrews McMeel Publishing, LLC

Kansas City • Sydney • London

Andrews McMeel Publishing, LLC
an Andrews McMeel Universal company
1130 Walnut Street, Kansas City, Missouri 64106

www.andrewsmcmeel.com

11 12 13 14 15 TEN 10 9 8 7 6 5 4 3 2 1

ISBN: 978-1-4494-0307-2

Library of Congress Control Number: 2010937879

ATTENTION: SCHOOLS AND BUSINESSES
Andrews McMeel books are available at quantity discounts with bulk purchase for educational, business, or sales
promotional use. For information, please e-mail the Andrews McMeel Publishing Special Sales Department:
specialsales@amuniversal.com

CONTENTS

FAIL

AT SCHOOL

2

FAIL

This Are The United States

4

FAIL

PANSY KIDD MIDDLE SCHOOL

FAIL

This is the map of Mexico.

7	3	9	2	4
+3	+5	+1	+3	+2

| 3 2 4 | 5 8 6 | 10 8 7 | 3 2 5 | 7 5 6 |

6	3	8	1	2
+2	+4		6	+1

| 7 8 4 | 7 8 | 8 | 8 7 | 1 2 3 |

6	2			4
+0	+4	+3	+6	+1

| 6 0 5 | 3 4 6 | 3 6 4 | 9 10 3 | 3 5 4 |

Friday: Read or listen to a favorite book. Review all sight words. Have a great weekend.

FAIL

FAIL

AT THE MALL

FAIL

18

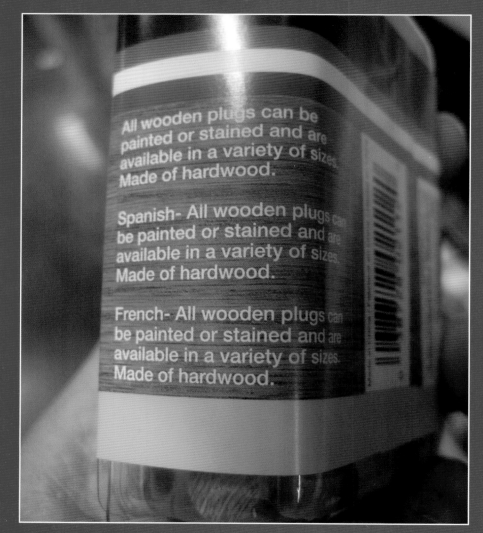

All wooden plugs can be painted or stained and are available in a variety of sizes. Made of hardwood.

Spanish- All wooden plugs can be painted or stained and are available in a variety of sizes. Made of hardwood.

French- All wooden plugs can be painted or stained and are available in a variety of sizes. Made of hardwood.

FAIL

19

FAIL

FAIL

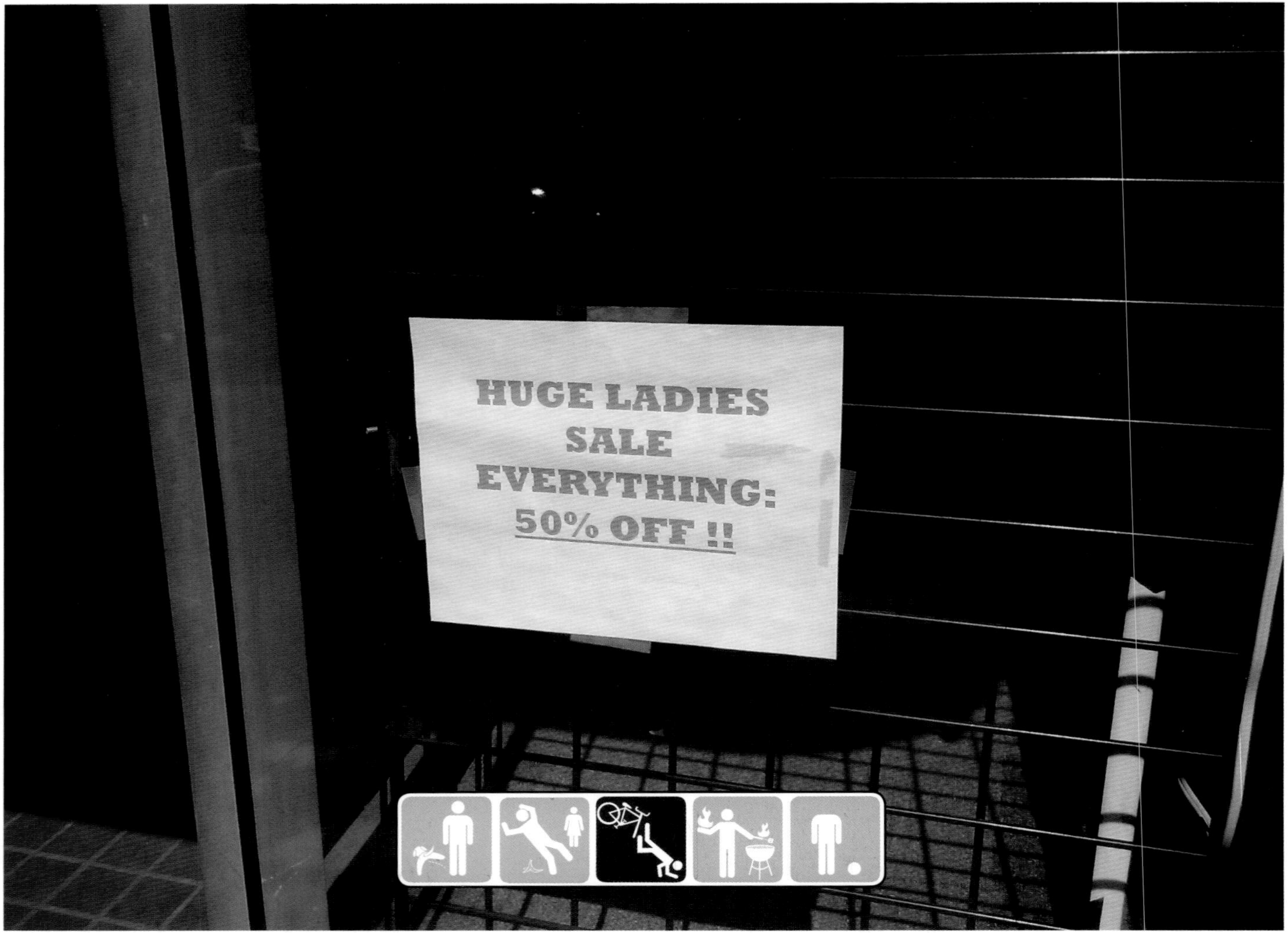
HUGE LADIES
SALE
EVERYTHING:
50% OFF !!

FAIL

FAIL

FAIL

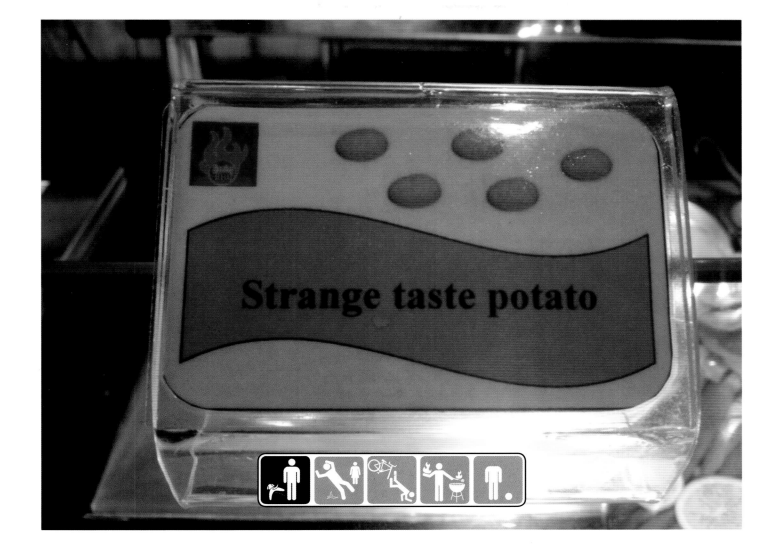

FAIL

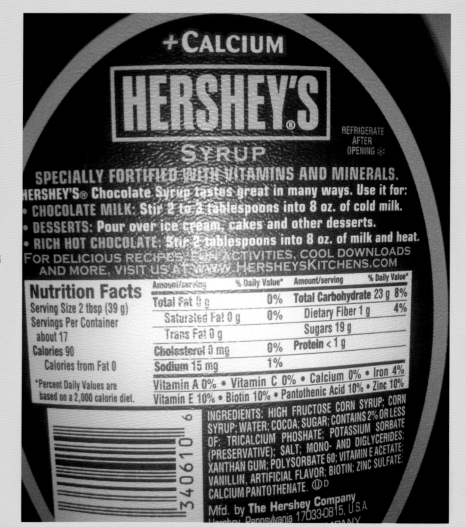

+CALCIUM

HERSHEY'S®

SYRUP

REFRIGERATE
AFTER
OPENING ❄

SPECIALLY FORTIFIED WITH VITAMINS AND MINERALS.

HERSHEY'S® Chocolate Syrup tastes great in many ways. Use it for:
• CHOCOLATE MILK: Stir 2 to 3 tablespoons into 8 oz. of cold milk.
• DESSERTS: Pour over ice cream, cakes and other desserts.
• RICH HOT CHOCOLATE: Stir 2 tablespoons into 8 oz. of milk and heat.
FOR DELICIOUS RECIPES, FUN ACTIVITIES, COOL DOWNLOADS
AND MORE, VISIT US AT WWW.HERSHEYSKITCHENS.COM

36

Nutrition Facts

Serving Size 2 tbsp (39 g)
Servings Per Container
about 17
Calories 90
Calories from Fat 0

*Percent Daily Values are
based on a 2,000 calorie diet.

Amount/serving	% Daily Value*	Amount/serving	% Daily Value*
Total Fat 0 g	0%	Total Carbohydrate 23 g	8%
Saturated Fat 0 g	0%	Dietary Fiber 1 g	4%
Trans Fat 0 g		Sugars 19 g	
Cholesterol 0 mg	0%	Protein < 1 g	
Sodium 15 mg	1%		

Vitamin A 0% • Vitamin C 0% • Calcium 0% • Iron 4%
Vitamin E 10% • Biotin 10% • Pantothenic Acid 10% • Zinc 10%

INGREDIENTS: HIGH FRUCTOSE CORN SYRUP; CORN
SYRUP; WATER; COCOA; SUGAR; CONTAINS 2% OR LESS
OF: TRICALCIUM PHOSHATE; POTASSIUM SORBATE
(PRESERVATIVE); SALT; MONO- AND DIGLYCERIDES;
XANTHAN GUM; POLYSORBATE 60; VITAMIN E ACETATE;
VANILLIN, ARTIFICIAL FLAVOR; BIOTIN; ZINC SULFATE;
CALCIUM PANTOTHENATE. Ⓤ Ⓓ

Mfd. by **The Hershey Company**
Hershey, Pennsylvania 17033-0815, U.S.A.

FAIL

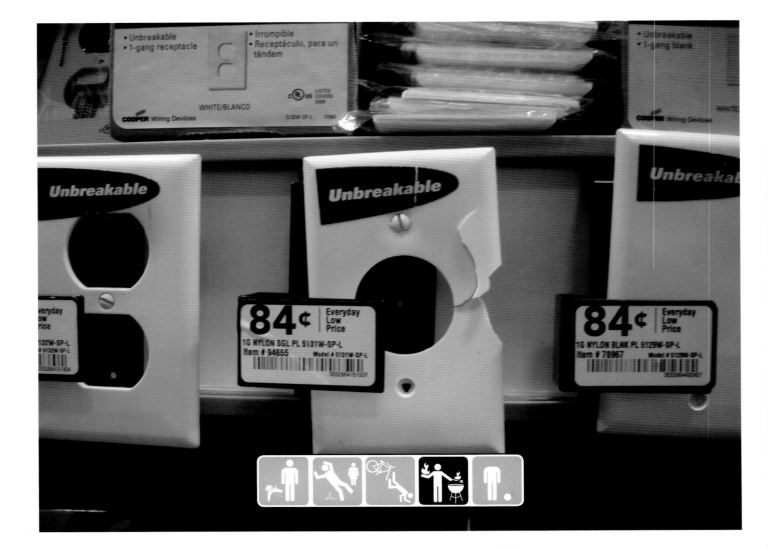

FAIL

FAIL
FOR THE HOLIDAYS

FAIL

Decorative Posable Bat With 8 ft Wing Span and Battery Operated LED Eyes

FAIL

NAME teen Girl

AGE teen CODE 2009teen

GIFT SUGGESTIONS NOTED BELOW

TOY/GIFT_____

GIFT SET_____

GIFT CARD_____

SHIRT/BLOUSE_____SWEATER_____

DESCRIPTION hand held

toy & Batteries

JESUS HATES

| EASTER | EASTER | EASTER |
| EGGS | BASKETS | BUNNIES |

PAGAN GODS OF SEX

CROSS BEARER MINISTRY LARRY ADAMS

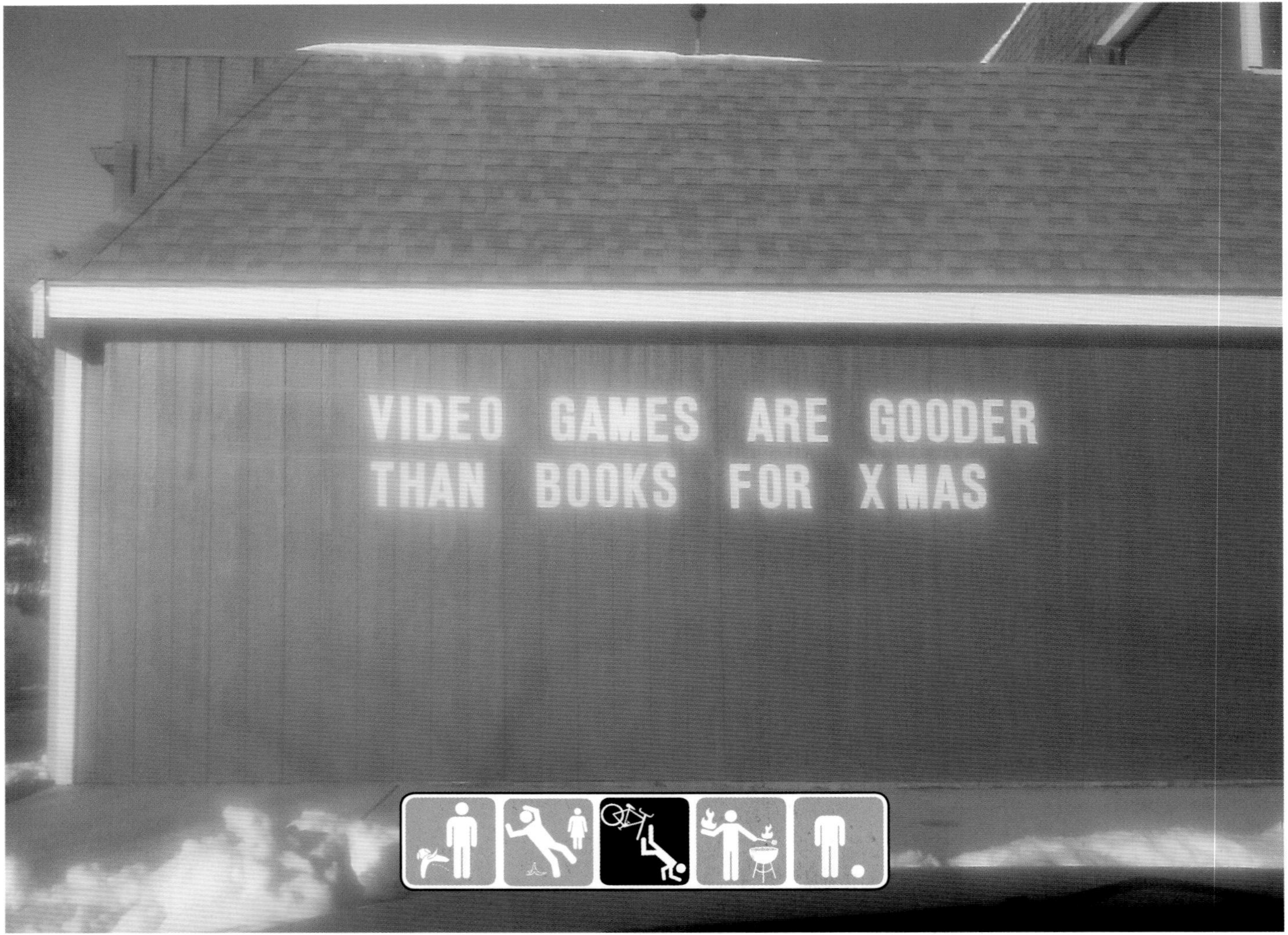
VIDEO GAMES ARE GOODER
THAN BOOKS FOR XMAS

FAIL

FAIL

FAIL

IN A RELATIONSHIP

FAIL

You will experience small success, especially in romance.

$ add cheese, american   5.49

                          Sub Total: 25.12
                               Tax: 1.26
12/10 8:12p TOTAL: 26.38

((HAVING AN AFFAIR?))
CATERING IS OUR SPECIALTY
(703)
** PLEASE PAY YOUR SERVER **

FAIL

FAIL

ROMANTIC GAZEBO

Enjoy . . . .
The romance of surrounding rice field view with
a beautiful Romantic Dinner, cocked just for you
by our Talented Chef.
Served elegantly on Romantic Gazebo
performing by Duo Musician

USD 65 nett / person

FAIL

FAIL

66

FAIL

IN THE NEIGHBORHOOD

FAIL

71

FAIL

74

FAIL

FAIL

FAIL

CHECK OUT OUR
LAYAWAY
PLAN

Bill's
dollar store

FAIL

FAIL

FAIL

ANTIQUE TABLES
MADE DAILY
1-800-

FOR SALE

OPEN HOUSE

OPEN HOUSE

FAIL

FAIL

IN YOUR FREE TIME

Closed to
Fishing

FAIL

FAIL

DESCRIPTION/FUNCTION	PHONE NUMBER
GENERAL INFORMATION GRADUATED DRIVER LICENSE SUBSTANCE ABUSE PROGRAM COMPLETIONS	
TRAFFIC CITATION OR COURT RELATED ACTIONS COMMERCIAL DRIVER LICENSE MEDICAL REVIEW BOARD	
STATE TRAFFIC SCHOOL HEARINGS FRAUD INS	

COMING INTO
THIS OFFICE TO
MAKE A
PAYMENT ON
YOUR DUI FINE
WITH ALCOHOL
ON YOUR BREATH
IS NOT A GOOD
IDEA

FAIL

FAP IN REAR OF ROSS 975-D

FAIL

FAIL

Le Petit Mort

Psychic Fair

Cancelled

due to unforeseen
circumstances

FAIL
ON THE JOB

FAIL

Please,
Make sure
the door is
unlocked
before
leaving!
Thank You

!Caution!
Door Does
Not Lock

FAIL

114

FAIL

Attention Male Dancers

On Thursday nights, you will be sharing the downstairs bathroom with *Girl Scouts*.

Please take care to change behind the curtains that have been provided for you, and to check to see that the bathroom is empty before you use the facilities.

Thank you for your assistance.

115

FAIL

FAIL

FAIL
ON YOUR ROAD TRIP

FAIL

CRISIS COUNSELING

THERE IS HOPE
MAKE THE CALL

THE CONSEQUENCES OF
JUMPING FROM THIS
BRIDGE ARE FATAL
AND TRAGIC.

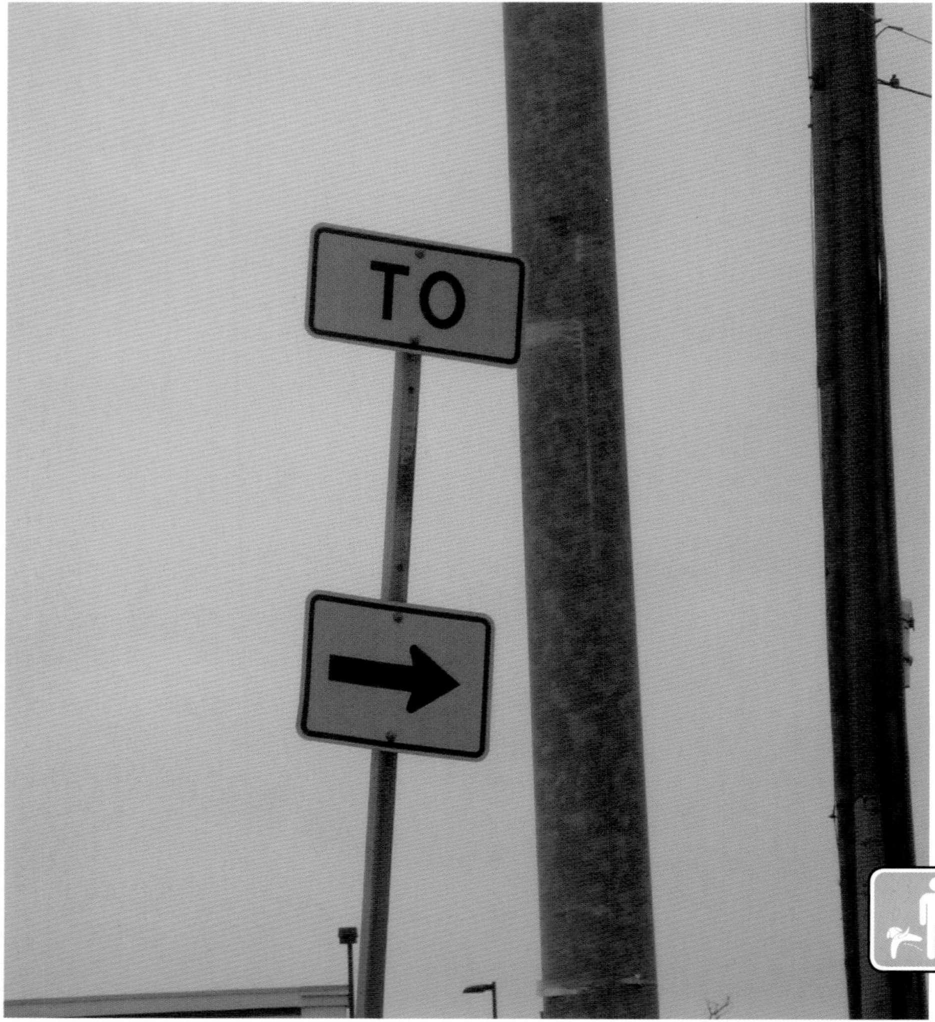

FAIL

FAIL

FAIL

FAIL

DICK BLISS PARK

36 YEARS OF DEDICATED SERVICE

FROM 1933 TO 1969

FAIL

FAIL

S. MARCO
RIALTO
←

S. MARCO
RIALTO
→

AFFITTACAMERE
CA' DARIO →

FAIL

FAIL

THIS BRIDGE IS PROVIDED BY THE SUTLIFF BRIDGE AUTHORITY. ENJOY IT AT YOUR OWN RISK!

No feeding animals.
請勿誘食

FAIL

143

FAIL

FAIL

WARNING

IT IS A
FEDERAL
OFFENSE TO
DISTURB
HARASS
OR MOLEST
SEALS

STAY WELL
BACK FROM
THE SEALS

FAIL

150

FAIL

FAIL

FAIL
WITH YOUR KIDS

FAIL

美洲虎籠舍
Jaguar Enclosure

兒童遊樂場
Children's Playground

160

FAIL

FAIL

FAIL

IMPORTANT NOTICE!
ALL ADULTS ARE RESTRICTED
FROM PLAYING ON JUMPS.

Do Not Enter
Without adult supervision

FAIL

Kingston Hospital **NHS**
NHS Trust

Be Kind to the Fish

Please do not let children <u>bang</u> on the fish tank. This will harm or even <u>kill</u> them (FISH).

Please remember

FAIL

FAIL
WITH YOUR PETS

FAIL

CAT LEACH

178

FAIL

CREDITS

PRODUCTION CREDITS

Editing: Sonya Vatomsky, Todd Sawicki, and Ben Huh
FAIL Scale Illustrations: Emily Nokes

IMAGE CREDITS

FAIL at School

page 2: Fuzzy Dice Pimp—shout out to ASGI Forums
page 3: Mopeychild
page 4: Red and the Joe's garage brigade
page 5: talzini and kellyO
page 6: Philip R. Hines and Stephen M. Hines
page 7: Emily Mattucci
page 8: Hillary (apictureandfivehundredwords.blogspot.com)
page 9: Daniel Matthews
page 10: Ed Mason
page 11: Cole and Holly Livingston

FAIL at the Mall

page 14: Stephen Bell
page 15: Jordan Smith and Robin Papak, partners in crime and experts in hotness
page 16: Noah Taylor

page 17: William Chui and Christina Tang
page 18: Chrissy Maron
page 19: Andy Smith (a.k.a. General Anubis)
page 20: Composer and musician Diwa de Leon (www.diwadeleon.com)
page 21: Troy Doerner—I saw my chance, so I took it. Don't cry because you didn't have the balls to fight.
page 22: Discovered by Sean and Ven; Photo by dj
page 23: Jon Markman—Ann Arbor, Michigan
page 24: Allen Kevorkov—Lancaster, Pennsylvania, www.AllenKevorkov.com
page 25: Mary Ann Dix and Richard Moss
page 26: Ramzi A., our Failman from Amsterdam
page 27: Yolanda Steller, C.R.!!
page 28: Justin and Melissa Evans
page 29: Caleb K. Matthiesen—Seattle '10
page 30: Danny Huizinga (and thanks to Taylor for showing me failblog!)
page 31: Photo: Mark Fox; Inspiration: College Park's finest
page 32: Ryan Hawkins and the Hawkins Family
page 33: Maff Jackson
page 34: Edie Rowner /Howard Rowner (facebook.com/GeekyGourmet)
page 35: Naomi Rubin (www.naomiyaki.com)
page 36: Midnyte

FAIL with Your Kids

FAIL with Your Pets